SO-ASE-769

COVERING WASHINGTON:
A GUIDEBOOK FOR REPORTERS

BILL GERTZ

Center for Security Policy Press
securefreedom.org

BOOKS BY BILL GERTZ

Betrayal: *How the Clinton Administration
Undermined American Security*

The China Threat:
How the People's Republic Targets America

Breakdown: *How America's Intelligence
Failures Led to September 11*

Treachery: *How America's Friends and Foes
Are Secretly Arming Our Enemies*

Enemies: *How America's Foes Steal
Our Vital Secrets—and How We Let It Happen*

The Failure Factory:
*How Unelected Bureaucrats, Liberal Democrats
and Big Government Republicans
Are Undermining America's Security
and Leading Us to War*

COVERING WASHINGTON:
A GUIDEBOOK FOR REPORTERS

BILL GERTZ

Center for Security Policy Press
securefreedom.org

© 2011 Bill Gertz

All rights reserved.

Covering Washington: A Guidebook for Reporters
is a National Security and New Media Journalism
Monograph, and is published in the United States by the Center
for Security Policy Press, a division of
the Center for Security Policy.

For more information, see securefreedom.org

ISBN 978-0-9850292-0-3

Printed in the United States of America

CONTENTS

ABOUT THE AUTHOR

Bill Gertz is an internationally recognized journalist who has been reporting the news since 1977. He currently writes the weekly Inside the Ring column for *The Washington Times* and is Senior Editor at *The Washington Free Beacon*, specializing in national and international security affairs. He is the author of six books, four of them national bestsellers. His latest book, *The Failure Factory*, about government bureaucracy and national security, was published in September 2008.

Mr. Gertz has an international reputation. Vyachaslav Trubnikov, head of the Russian Foreign intelligence service, once called him a "tool of the CIA" after he wrote an article exposing Russian intelligence operations in the Balkans. A senior CIA official also threatened to have a cruise missile fired at his desk at The Washington Times after he wrote a column critical of the CIA's analysis on China. The state-run Xinhua news agency in 2006 identified Mr. Gertz as the No. 1 "anti-China expert" in the world. For the record, Mr. Gertz insists he is very much pro-China—pro-Chinese people but he opposes the Chinese communist system.

Former Defense Secretary Donald H. Rumsfeld once told him: "You are drilling holes in the Pentagon and sucking out information," a comment he did not intend as a compliment.

Mr. Gertz studied English literature at Washington College in Chestertown, Md., and journalism at George Washington University, Washington, D.C. He is married and has two daughters.

PREFACE

This monograph is a product of the National Security and New Media Journalism Project of the Center for Security Policy. The Project seeks to develop and promote the craft of journalism with an emphasis on national security affairs.

Since the September 11 attacks on the United States, news reporting on national security affairs has taken on a new urgency as reporters, editors and producers often find themselves grappling with new issues related to foreign threats, and reporting on sensitive news and information that are part of the undeclared but deadly war on terrorism, along with other issues such as nuclear arms proliferation and arms control, the growing threat posed by the People's Republic of China, and Russia's gradual reversion into an anti-democratic state.

Many journalists today are ill equipped and inadequately trained to understand and report on these important news areas. The news industry no longer seems to appreciate the value of clear and accurate reporting on U.S. national security affairs and foreign policies. Too often, news reports end up sensationalizing or trivializing these critical issues. As a result there has been a historic dumbing down of news that ill-serves the American public and ultimately weakens U.S. national security. If we cannot fully understand the nature of the threats facing the country, then we will be hard-pressed to find workable solutions and effective policies to counter them.

Few reporters today have the background, expertise and understanding of critical national security issues required to report effectively on the subject. Worse, there are signs of increasing bias among journalists who often promote value-neutral and politically-correct news that is undermining the American system of government while ill-serving both American and foreign publics.

To counteract these trends, the Center for Security Policy established the National Security and New Media Journalism Project. The goal of the Project is to focus the debate on these trends in news reporting, and work towards new standards for accuracy and integrity in national security journalism.

To learn more about the project, please visit nationalsecurityjournalism.org

INTRODUCTION

During a regular haircut at my local barbershop, the conversation shifted to what I do for a living. After explaining my job as a newspaper reporter who covers Washington, DC, the barber asked: "Oh, have you met the president?" "No but I read his mail," I replied.

The exchange captures my career as a Washington newspaper reporter for over 30 years covering the government bureaucracy.

The mail in question was the basis of a November 7, 1997 article with the headline: "Yeltsin Letter Reveals Anti-Satellite Weapons." It was based on a private letter that began "Dear Bill" and was signed "B. Yeltsin." An English translation had found its way to my possession shortly after it was sent by Russian President Boris Yeltsin to President Bill Clinton. Moscow, according to Yeltsin, opposed what Yeltsin said were U.S. plans to develop a "whole gamut of anti-satellite weapons." And, it revealed this key news nugget: Russia "at one time... possessed an anti-satellite capability"—and therefore probably still does today.

The White House spokesman at the time, Mike McCurry, reacted stoically to what was just one of a torrent of similar leaks of inside information that came from the ship of state. A year earlier, I had disclosed another extraordinary exchange between Clinton and Yeltsin at a summit meeting, where Clinton, ever the shameless politician, sought to coax Yeltsin into lifting a ban on U.S. chicken exports sold by Clinton's Arkansas friends at Tyson's chicken. The disclosure prompted the Russian government to call in the U.S. Ambassador to Russia to protest what the Foreign Ministry said were "provocative" leaks to the press.

"The president ought to be able have a private conversation," was how then-White House Press Secretary Mike McCurry responded to the leaks. Of the Yeltsin-Clinton anti-satellite letter, McCurry noted that such correspondence is normally classified "Secret."

As a news reporter, obviously, I have a different perspective. Inside information such as that revealed in the private exchanges between high-ranking government officials is the lifeblood of a free press independent of government control. For me as a reporter working in Washington I firmly believe that such press freedom, however uncomfortable for the government, remains vital to the national security of the United States.

Working in Washington as a news reporter has been an absolutely incredible experience. If I were to walk away from the news business today, I would have no regrets. The things I have seen, the reports I have written, and places I have traveled made for a truly amazing journalism—and life—experience. I have traveled with secretaries of defense on scores of trips. On one in the late 1990s, I flew aboard a rickety Soviet-era helicopter with a group of reporters and defense officials to a former strategic missile base in central Russia. We watched in amazement as an old ICBM in its silo, once targeted on American cities, was blown up as part of a disarmament program. During a visit to the Central Asian state of Uzbekistan, my questioning of the president during a national television interview on why Uzbek opposition political figures were disappearing at the hands of his government's agents nearly caused an international incident. The local U.S. ambassador at the time told me Uzbek government officials were so upset they wanted me detained. The U.S. ambassador was told by the Uzbeks I was lucky to be getting out of the country.

On another adventurous reporting experience, our Pentagon press reporters flew non-stop from Andrews Air Force Base near Washington to Kuala Lumpur, Malaysia aboard an Air Force E-4, a militarized Boeing 747 used as an airborne command post—if there were a nuclear war. The aircraft refueled twice in mid-air on the way.

During a visit to an Air Force special operations base, I fired a high-speed "minigun" ultra-rapid fire machine gun from the window of a Pave Hawk helicopter at night over a firing range in Florida. The gun had two speeds: fast and faster. How fast? Between 2,000 and 6,000 rounds per minute.

But travel is just one of the perks of the news business.

In Washington, my ability to produce news stories based on inside information made me both a hero and a target. For example, access to details of missile defense negotiations with the Russians during the 1990s so frustrated senior U.S. officials that a new level of the "Secret" information classification category was created just to keep me out. It was called "Secret-Prose." Others dubbed it the "No Gertz" compartment.

The point is that news reporting, in addition to being difficult work, can also be incredible fun.

This monograph is for journalists who want to work in Washington, where government and politics are the major industry. The principles and rules discussed, are focused on national security reporting but are applicable to all facets of the news business here and in other locales.

1. WHAT IS THE GOAL
OF NEWS REPORTING?

Simply put, the journalist's goal is to tell the truth. In reporting and editing, reporters provide news to readers, viewers or listeners. Telling the truth is neither simple nor easy. It requires gathering facts, understanding complex circumstances and ferreting out information that is often hidden or blocked from public disclosure.

For our purposes, the dictionary defines news, according to Merriam Webster, as "a report of recent events" and "previously unknown information." In reality, news is anything a news organization believes its readers want to read, along with information they need. News can range widely from the status of the Washington Redskins' quarterback prior to a game, to the internal workings of a Pentagon committee set up to make large-scale defense budget cuts.

There are two general types of reporting: one is breaking news and the other is enterprise reporting. Breaking news can be the public testimony of a secretary of defense or state, a White House announcement of a new policy, or report by a think tank. To compete effectively with other news outlets, reporters need to develop knowledge of the subject to be able to identify any and all new angles or nuances that will produce a news lede for a story.

As a new reporter in the 1980s, this was one of the more difficult aspects of the news business for me to learn. Before being able to quickly identify the most important element of a public event I was covering, I relied on editors or wire service dispatches to help writing ledes. I eventually learned to answer the question, "what is the most important news element of this?" or "what here has not been reported before?" or "although nothing was new, is there something here that is under-reported?"

Sometimes there just isn't any news and then, in consultation with editors, it was decided not to produce a story.

News is shaped by the editors who run news organizations. Priorities are placed by them on different news areas, such as politics, national security affairs, foreign reporting, domestic financial issues, long-term investigative reporting, etc. Editors provide guidance and most times make assignments for stories to be covered. Reporters need to communicate and work closely with their editors so that they are clear on what kind of news stories are sought.

2. WHAT KIND OF PERSON MAKES A GOOD JOURNALIST?

The news business is people-oriented. All aspects of news reporting require good people skills. Talking, listening and most important, questioning. At all stages of news production, from editors who assign stories, to reporters who gather the facts, to sources who provide information, to experts who comment on those facts and information, constant people-to-people interaction is a fundamental part of the job. Being able to work with people is an essential attribute for a successful journalist. But do not worry too much if you lack confidence in ability to interact with people. People skills can be learned and get better with experience.

Producing news stories is a collaborative process and good news reporters require good editors. The various editors (producers in broadcast) function as the make judgments about whether certain news is worth reporting at all, or whether a story is a major news story with a banner headline or an article that gets less play through placement inside the newspaper. Senior editors generally set overall strategic policy for news coverage. Desk editors have a more hands on role in working with reporters. And reporters are the fontline troops in the field who cover news and help find news.

One of the most important characteristics of a successful journalist is a constant questioning attitude. What is the most important aspect of a certain event? What is this person saying? What is it about this information that I need to understand to be able to convey it to readers in a news story?

One Washington reporter compared the journalist's job to one of the various intelligence functions. In intelligence, the various types of intelligence are called "-ints," short for intelligence. The two main ones are "humint," short for human intelligence, and "sigint" for signals, or electronic intelligence.

For journalists, one of the more successful forms of information gathering has been dubbed "Ask-int." Ask questions, and keep asking questions, and the answers you get will help you produce news. Remember there may be dumb answers, but there are few dumb questions. Ask a question and you never know what the answer will be.

I am amazed at how effective this simple technique works for journalists, especially in the Washington news-gathering milieu. Ask questions and keep asking questions. Many times you won't get a good answer. But many times you will.

So how does a reporter develop a questioning demeanor? That can be done by working hard to learn and understand the subject of the news you are covering. The Internet can be a great tool in this. But you must be cautious in accepting at face value what is on the Internet. Wikipedia can be useful for checking certain facts, like dates and basic data. A better tool is to use your news organization's archive. This is an essential part of news reporting because it is important to know what has been reported before. Oftentimes reporters end up re-writing stories published earlier that contain most of the same information because they did not take the time to check the archives. Most news archives today are digitized and thus easier to access than in the days when newspapers had only paper clippings in the newspaper's morgue of old stories.

3. GET IT FIRST,
BUT GET IT RIGHT

The news business is very competitive. Hundreds and even thousands of news reporters cover Washington on a daily basis. All are out for the same things: covering various branches of government and the private sector. All are looking for news for their readers, viewers or listeners. In Washington, the wire services and major newspapers have the largest staffs. Most news organizations subscribe or belong to wire services. The main wires are Associated Press and Reuters News Agency. Agence France Presse is a third, and Bloomberg is an up and coming, mainly business-oriented news service. Many of these services stories are available without subscription on the Internet. Be wary of foreign government-controlled news services like Xinhua, the state-run Chinese news service (whose foreign correspondents, according to U.S. intelligence officials, are mainly Chinese intelligence officers), or Itar-Tass, the Russian news agency.

The competitive nature of the news business means that reporters are often under pressure to produce stories. Deadlines are part of the business. But deadline pressure should never become an excuse for not getting your story correct. In Washington, getting it first is an imperative. Getting the story right is absolute requirement. Do not let the pressure of trying to keep a story an exclusive for your news organization compromise adherence to journalistic standards.

This is an ironclad rule of news reporting. Avoid at all costs being wrong. That said, mistakes happen. And some mistakes are worse and more costly than others. Always be prepared to run corrections when you find mistakes, errors and inaccuracies. More often, someone else will call your attention to errors in your stories. In my career, I have experienced my share of errors. The way to handle an error is learn from your mistakes, move on and vow to yourself that it will not happen again. Names and other misspellings are one area you must use care. Never expect an editor or copyeditor to catch your mistakes.

Technical errors are one thing. Errors of fact are another. It is a given that you must make sure you have the facts straight. Err on the side of caution. When in doubt, leave it out, or wait until you can verify it. Never plagiarize, something journalistically akin to theft. If you must use facts reported in only one other place, it is important to give credit where credit it due. When picking up material from other news reports, limit what you use and tell the reader that it was first reported in a specific publication or new outlet.

Before publishing a news story, in the course of reporting, try to learn whether other news outlets have the same or similar story and whether they will be reporting on what you plan to report. You can ask official sources if they know of other news organizations that are working on a similar story. By protocol, official news sources, mainly public affairs officials, are not supposed to inform other reporters if they have knowledge of other reporters' news stories or have helped different reporters. But sometimes they will tell you and other times their answer can give you a hint.

If you have an exclusive story that you feel confident no other news organization has, be aware that you must not tip off the competition to your scoop.

In the real world, there are unscrupulous officials who will seek to undermine you. Sometimes, sources, both official and unofficial, notify other reporters about your story—to be spiteful or to undermine your news organization for their own reasons—and you could lose the exclusive. Always strive first and foremost for accuracy and fairness in producing your story. But also be aware of whether you will "lose" the exclusivity of your story to other news outlets. Getting beat on stories is something all good reporters try to avoid.

But don't go to extremes. Remember, there are always other stories out there. If you lose one exclusive to the opposition, forget about it (but remember if it was compromised by a source) and move on to other stories. There are always other good and sometimes high-impact news stories out there waiting for you find.

4. THE PUBLIC AFFAIRS BUREAUCRACY

Washington reporting requires you to frequently interact with government and private sector officials who are part of public affairs offices. The private sector frequently uses public relations firms to handle corporate and non-government entity media relations under contract.

Always remember that these public affairs people are the official part of the story and generally are motivated in the direction of limiting public disclosure about a certain news event, usually to protect a company or agency, or more likely, their seniormost officials.

One of the first steps for reporters covering Washington: Contact relevant public affairs offices. Introduce yourself to the office and find out who works the office and whether there are specific people assigned to handle your questions, inquiries and issues. Collect and log their email, telephone numbers and other data. Keeping good records on these people is essential. Public affairs people tend to move to new positions frequently and it is important to keep track of who moves on and who comes aboard.

Public affairs officials act as mediators between the press and the officials in government agencies. These "flacks," as they are often called, vary widely in their utility to news reporters, typically running the gamut from highly professional, pro-media types who are helpful and as a result can be excellent new sources, to some who in the extreme, are outright liars who regard the press as enemies and seemingly delight in providing reporters with false or more often, misleading information.

The public affairs system at one time was disjointed and unconnected. When I began covering Washington in the 1980s, it was fairly easy to obtain bits and pieces of information from public affairs officials in one agency and take that information to other agencies' public affairs officials to gain more.

With advances in communications technology, however, today's public affairs offices are highly organized and tightly controlled, often at the White House level for government agencies, press operations that seek to limit the dissemination of information, whether based on political or policy imperatives. For example, most administrations dispatch political appointees to public affairs offices to be ready to alert senior officials outside that agency to news reports that have the potential for creating political fallout for the president or his cabinet officials or other senior officials.

Public affairs officials are trained or directed to be helpful toward reporters for certain news stories that are considered beneficial to the agency. However, often times, they are directed to be unhelpful when news stories potentially will create problems, such as triggering legal, inspector general, or congressional investigations, or just bad publicity.

This can be done using a number of mechanisms. Most flacks are trained to avoid using the words "no comment," that in today's information age can be tantamount to confirmation, although as a reporter you can't accept that as confirmation of something you are reporting. Today, the clever answer to a reporter's question is something to the effect "I don't have anything for you" to which your next question should be "Why not?" The person usually just repeats the same response.

Flacks almost always insist that no reporter directly contact someone in their agency without first going through the public affairs office. This is a reflection of bureaucratic turf that is closely guarded, and is generally a way to control the flow of information to the press. I generally ignore this rule and whenever possible contact the person I need to speak with directly, usually via email or phone. Email is generally easier.

One constant annoyance is one of the most frequent responses from flacks in response to inquiry: "What is your deadline?" I've learned over the years that this is a manipulative device used to determine when the reporter needs the information, ostensibly so that the public affairs office can answer your inquiry based on a request to know when you need the information. In reality asking for deadlines is usually a subterfuge for finding out when the story will appear in print, broadcast on online and whether flack has to sound the alarm to higher authority.

Also, knowing your deadline in some cases can be used to delay publication, if the public affairs officer is able to determine that your story cannot run before they provide a response and is thus dependent on their response.

Technically, a reporter's deadline is part of a reporting process that generally is not to be shared with people outside a news organization. And thus deadlines should not be disclosed to public affairs officers because that knowledge can be used to influence the news process.

Practically, telling flacks your deadline must be weighed within the context of your story. If you have an exclusive that is in danger of being lost to competing news organizations, it is generally a good practice to seek out official comment later in the news gathering processes, to avoid the story from being circulated within government and thus being leaked to competitors. I have responded to this deadline question in several ways. In some cases I inform flacks that my deadline is none of their business, something that generally is not a good idea. But by contrast, saying you don't have a deadline means the person can file your query in the trash, or delay you for several days.

On other occasions I have said I need the information by 5:00 p.m. or 6:00 p.m. or "close of business today." A middle ground is to explain: "I need the information as soon as possible."

One reason for not being specific about a deadline is that you might think your deadline is a certain time on that day, only to have editors or others hold the story for any number of reasons, such as gathering more facts and details, expanding comment on the topic or simply because there isn't space that day (for print newspapers, mainly).

Regardless of the type of public affairs officials you encounter, always be polite and professional. Remember that when reporting you are a representative of your news organization and need to put personal feelings aside. I rarely violate this rule. When I have, it was in response to excessively rude, insulting and unprofessional behavior on the part of a flack. Avoid this, but should it occur, immediately notify your editor or supervisor to explain what happened.

And always remember one of the cardinal rules of Washington culture: Only amateurs stay angry. Why? Because you never know when a particular person will be important for your news gathering and reporting in the future.

Government agencies vary greatly in their approach to the press. Some are starved for news coverage and as a result tend to be very helpful if they think a reporter is writing anything about them. Others involved in controversial policies and programs are defensive and view the press as the enemy to be spun or blocked.

Most have professional people who will "staff" your questions and inquiries, a process that can be slow and inefficient. Some request that you submit your question in writing, usually through an email or fax.

One case study: The Department of Defense. It operates a large public affairs office with as many as 50 people who deal with the press. In addition, each military service has its own public affairs office and many defense agencies also have separate press operations, as do often far-flung military commands and operations.

The multiple offices are often used to duck questions. Officials, in typical government bureaucratic fashion, will tell reporters, "You need to call" someone other than the person you are talking to. This can be a sincere request, but more often it is a bureaucrat's way of not having to work the question. One reporter described the Pentagon's pass-the-buck culture in public affairs by noting that if you ask a Pentagon flack what time it is, he will tell you to call Switzerland because they make watches. Another long-time defense reporter said he believes that many public affairs officials spend their time thinking about how they can lie or dissemble in responses to reporters' questions.

The best solution for this problem is develop solid reliable sources outside the official public affairs bureaucracy. For a reporter, the best position to be in prior to calling public affairs for comment or help is to have all the facts nailed down. Knowing the facts cold is the best way to know or anticipate the official response to your questions, usually from information imparted to you on a background, not-for-attribution basis.

The background information system is a long-time vehicle used in Washington to provide information to reporters without linking it to a person or agency by name. The general rule is that you, as a reporter, are interacting with people in an on-the-record fashion as soon as you identify yourself as a news reporter representing a news organization and seeking information. Background for unofficial sources is the granting of confidentiality to a person so that the person is not the target of reprisal for disclosing the information. The government, for its own reasons, has made this easier by providing certain information on background, usually through briefings, without attribution to officials by name. A third level is off-the-record. Off the record means you cannot use the information for publication, a level of confidentiality that should be used in the most stringent of circumstances. After all, why agree to allow someone to give you information you can't report? You are a news reporter and want material you can publish. Off the record is often used by government officials when a reporter has information that is false but that providing the correct information would violate secrecy rules. Other uses for off the record are that people want to give information but do not want to see it in print. The government does this to "inform" reporters. Are reporters forbidden to take off-the-record information to other sources and then get it moved up the news food chain to background? There are no hard and fast rules on these and ambiguity is best left to the reporters' imagination.

5. NEWS SOURCES

It is a maxim of Washington news reporting that reporters are only as good as their sources. Identifying, contacting, cultivating and protecting news sources are fundamental for success.

And the success of a journalism career can be directly related to a reporter's success in developing, cultivating—and protecting—news sources.

My career as a national security affairs reporter in Washington is a direct result of developing and utilizing multiple, excellent sources of news. In past years, the type and amount of inside information I was able to obtain was truly extraordinary, as careful reading of the appendixes of several of my books will attest. I do not mean to brag, but simply point out that sources are the key. I remember one of my reporter colleagues calling an official I knew and asking him, "How do I get on Bill Gertz's mailing list?" Translation: Will you give me some of the things that have made him a successful reporter.

During a visit to China with Defense Secretary William Cohen in July 2000, I attended a banquet at Beijing hotel that was attended by Lt. Gen. Xiong Guangkai, at the time the head of Chinese military intelligence. After the dinner, as I was leaving, Cohen told Xiong, half-jokingly, as he pointed to me: "This guy has access to more intelligence information than anyone I know." The comment was an exaggeration by someone who as secretary of defense had access to the nation's most important defense and intelligence secrets. But it captured what good news sources mean for a reporter.

In recent years, the U.S. government has cracked down hard on government officials who talk to the press, prosecuting several for leaks of information to the press. The crackdown was an expression of frustration by the government over so much inside information coming out in the news. And I believe it was calculated to make it harder for news reporters to develop unofficial contacts with government officials.

The effort to plug leaks has been only marginally successful. In 2010, the government suffered its worst information security failure in history when an Army soldier in Iraq, reportedly using his computer skills, managed to steal several hundred thousand classified government documents. Wikileaks, the anti-secrecy web site, posted over 250,000 internal Pentagon field reports from Iraq and Afghanistan, and State Department cables. The disclosure of the Iraq and Afghanistan documents truly was a criminal offense because the raw intelligence reports revealed the identities of Iraqi and Afghan agents who had risked their lives to provide intelligence, only to be disclosed and endangered by some of the extremists they were secretly working against.

The State Department documents, however, have proven to be a news reporter's bonanza, revealing an amazing range of subjects, such as how a Chinese Communist Party Politboro member ordered a cyber attack on Google because he was upset by what was produced about him from a Google search of his name.

Sources are mainly people. But they also can be people who provide documents. I once was provided a highly-classified government document revealing that a military coup was being planned in a South American country. At the time, I thought to myself, "What am I going to do with this?" I could have reported it as a classified document saying there was going to be a coup in a South American country, but what if there wasn't a coup after I reported there would be? And if I started doing the legwork and asking if anyone knows about it, the inquiry would have tipped off the government that I knew about it. In the end, I decided to make a few phone calls to see what kind of response I received. I then waited over the weekend before writing the story. During the two-day period I noted a South American news report that said some people had been arrested in a South American country that were plotting a coup. For me, it was not a story. Normally, I would have reported on it. But at the time I was getting so much other information on so many different foreign affairs and international security news topics that I decided to move on to another story. It was a luxury I could afford because I had the luxury of having extraordinary sources.

Among the potential pool of people who can be cultivated as news sources are government officials, first and foremost, then government contractors and former officials, especially those who recently left government or military service. Congress is perhaps the very best place to develop sources, both members and staff.

Because the United States is such a free and open society, often people come to reporters as their last line of defense. They may have already gone to their agency superviser with a problem, or Congress or the courts, but were unable to get any relief for the problem. Many times they will then reach out to news reporters as a last resort. Sometimes their information does not produce a story. But sometimes it does. Reporters rely on such volunteers. Try to develop these into sources. Be opportunistic.

Also, Washington conferences are great places to develop sources, especially at think tanks that often are holding-tanks for former or future officials waiting for an administration to switch parties. Go to some of the many conferences that are held in Washington on a daily basis. Meet officials, former officials and experts. Ask questions related to news stories you are covering or working. If the person you are asking doesn't know, ask them if they can tell you someone who does know. Such referrals can be key way to develop sources. Think tanks in Washington often are staffed by former officials and are home to many experts. Study all the think tanks and their people who can produce a wealth of good sources, as well as providing leads to other sources and new stories.

To develop sources, you need to meet people who have access to the information you need. I have lived in Washington, Virginia and Maryland since the 1970s and my experience has been that it seems like almost every other house is occupied by someone who works for government. In Maryland, the largest employer in the state is supersecret National Security Agency at Fort Meade. Government openness has evolved considerably since four decades ago. For a long time NSA officials were prohibited from identifying where they worked. Initially it was "I work for the government." Then things loosened a bit and they would say "I work for the Defense Department," technically accurate since NSA's budget is tucked within the Pentagon budget. Recently, they say "I work for NSA," but then quickly clam up.

For potential sources, remember "ask-int." Ask questions. The answers often produce news. I have been truly amazed over the fact that if you ask enough people, you eventually will get answers. It's like a door-to-door salesman. If you keep knocking on doors, you are eventually going to sell something. That is the way it works. In Washington if you ask long enough, you will get answers; there may be places with doors that won't be open, but if you are persistent you will get information just from asking.

Protect sources. A single news source can be the springboard to a successful career. Keep relations with sources professional. There is nothing wrong with being friendly and this can be a key to source development. But remember to keep things in perspective.

Sources provide information to reporters for a few reasons. One is what I call the "whistle-blower motivation." Someone feels they need to blow the whistle on corruption, illicit activity or wrongdoing. Listen carefully but always check things out. There is saying in news circles that a grizzled city editor once told a young reporter: "If your mother says she loves you, check it out." Always check things out.

A second motivation is the "debate motivation." This usually revolves around differences and debate over policies, whether about the wisdom of building a new weapons system, or budgets, such as where to cut spending or where to add it. Know the debates inside government and you are on the track to finding sources. Congress and the administration are constantly at odds, even when both parties are in power. Find the conflict and debate and it will produce news exclusives.

Be careful and avoid being scammed by unscrupulous sources. There have been cases (not involving me) where sources provided useful and accurate information on one, two, three or more occasions. But then these sources will provide false information to a reporter with the goal of undermining the reporter's or the news organization's credibility. And credibility in news reporting is everything. Newspapers and news organizations live and die based on their credibility. Build it and protect it by getting your stories right.

It is a general rule for most news organization that reporters must always seek out two independent sources of information for their news reporting. In reality, however, it is not always possible and practical sense needs to be applied. If your one source happens to be the deputy secretary of state—which has happened in my experience—then one source can be sufficient. Again, reporters and editors need to weigh whether the story is important enough to report with just one source, or whether to wait and find additional sourcing to verify the information. In some cases, I have waited months before being able to get a second source on a story.

Try to keep the news reporting craft in perspective. Don't fall in love with your story (or with your sources). Early in my career I would agonize that I would be unable to close the loop on a big story. But after years of reporting I realized that although it may be hard to let a lead for a story go, there are always other stories out there to go after. Remember this fisherman's adage: There are many fish in the sea. And for Washington reporters this is a truism: There are many news stories waiting to be reported.

Be careful using sensitive information obtained from sources. Not every detail of sensitive information needs to be reported. Once during the Reagan administration, CIA Director William Casey came to visit *The Washington Times*. He said the agency and other intelligence agencies were being hurt by leaks to reporters. He said he was visiting various news organizations to ask reporters and editors to voluntarily do more to help protect intelligence sources. He didn't demand it. He didn't threaten to prosecute reporters. He made a commonsense appeal. And it has largely been followed by most news organizations, who also were approached by Casey.

This is a no-brainer for human sources. No reporter should report something that potentially could get someone killed. It is just not worth it. However, how do you know if you are putting someone's life at risk? It is not easy, but the problems deserve introspection and caution. Seek help from outside experts who have experience with the kind of sensitive information you are going to report. It is difficult to know when something you report is a problem, so it is worth being cautious. Electronic intelligence is often a tougher call. If the information came from electronic intelligence, Casey told us to try and avoid saying so, as disclosing that the information you obtained is derived from intercepted communications could quickly result in that source being lost, if the target being listened to electronically discovers it. Use common sense in dealing with sensitive information and ask experts if you have questions.

6. CARVING OUT DISTINCTIVE NEWS COVERAGE

A key to success in news reporting is producing exclusive or distinctive news coverage. Reporters do not operate alone. Editors with experience must guide news coverage and provide a reality check on suggested news stories, the use of sources. and the information gathered. Working together, editors and reporters produce the key dynamic that helps carve out unique news coverage areas. This is the process used to produce distinctive news coverage and major impact news stories that will drive readers to your news publication.

Journalists need a clear understanding of the role of the press. The power of the press lies in the ability of news organizations to provide a check on government. America's Founding Fathers built the U.S. government based on an underlying skepticism of centralized power in government. Thus, they set up a system designed to balance power between the executive, legislative and judiciary branches. To provide a further check on power, the Founders went one step more and codified in the Bill of Rights the notion of a free press, independent of government control.

One of the responsibilities of news reporters is to provide a check on government power, one step beyond the

THE FIRST AMENDMENT

"Congress shall make no law respecting an establishment of religion, or prohibiting the free exercise thereof; or abridging the freedom of speech, or of the press; or the right of the people peaceably to assemble, and to petition the Government for a redress of grievances."

three branches. This function, in my experience, is a vital component of protecting American freedom, liberty and national security.

Wags often say that the job of news reporters is to comfort the afflicted and afflict the comfortable. In reality, it is an unfortunate fact of life that corruption and wrongdoing are present in all aspects of society. Journalists must take seriously their responsibility to serve the public good by exposing that. In reporting the news, cover the waterfront of breaking news. But always look for stories that that will have a major impact. Some of the most significant news reports have triggered law enforcement investigations into crimes or illicit activities, or congressional investigations of policies and procedures.

Certainly the zenith of the power of the press was the Watergate scandal, when FBI official W. Mark Felt covertly assisted *The Washington Post* in exposing the activities of the administration of President Richard M. Nixon. The coverage eventually led to Nixon's resignation amid calls for impeachment. Likewise, press reporting on President Bill Clinton led to his impeachment regarding his affair with White House intern Monica Lewinsky.

A good example from my experience occurred during the Clinton administration. *The Washington Times* was successful in producing high impact news coverage on the topic of U.S. missile defenses. The issue grew out of the fact that in the late 1990s, the U.S. military had suffered the largest single number of casualties during the 1991 Persian Gulf War, from an Iraqi short-range Scud missile that hit a U.S. military barracks near Dahran, Saudi Arabia. The strike killed 27 soldiers and wounded 98. After the war, the senior military leaders understood that there was an urgent need to build missile defenses against short-range Scuds.

Policy officials in the Clinton Administration, however—much like the Barak Obama administration—had adopted a pro-arms control policy toward defense. This outlook was the opposite of the Reagan administration strategy of 'Peace through Strength': deterring and dissuading adversaries by building up U.S. military and other power, following the disaster of the Jimmy Carter presidency.

Clinton administration officials instead adopted the policy of seeking peace through negotiations and arms control agreements. The U.S. military understood that an over-reliance on international arms control talks and agreements threatened their ability to protect deployed forces from what was a real and growing threat of ballistic and cruise missile attacks. Also, most military leaders understand that in many cases of global arms agreements, the United States is the only party that honestly negotiates and abides by international treaties and accords. U.S. adversaries and negotiating partners approach arms talks differently. They often regard arms control pacts as a way to constrain or limit U.S. power. The result is usually agreements that restrict the United States and allow other nations to violate the treaties with impunity. I have observed this first hand on many occasions in covering defense affairs. For example, when Russia's government and military violated arms agreements with the United States, pro-arms control officials would dismiss the cheating a "militarily insignificant," as if the cheating was irrelevant. The reason: these officials did not want to undermine the *process* of arms control, which they regard as more important than any potential national security dangers from faulty arms agreements.

In the case of short-range missile defenses, the Clinton administration sought in negotiations with Russia to extend the provisions of 1972 the Anti-Ballistic Missile Treaty, or ABM treaty, that limited long-range missile defenses. They sought include restrictions on short-range defenses within the ABM Treaty. The military opposed the effort based on the Dharan barracks missile attack. U.S. troops had died from a short-range missile attack. They did not want to give up in an arms agreement the ability build the most effective short range missile defenses in a legally binding treaty.

The reason this line of reporting (which went on for most of the final years of the Clinton administration) produced news was that it was a reporting area that involved a conflict over policy. In looking for a story, try to find a debate or conflict over policy, or even the anticipation of conflict; it will almost always produce good news stories.

Missile defense was a difficult news topic to cover. The reporting involved understanding very technical terms like interceptor speeds and warhead velocities and then making those issues clear and understandable for newspaper readers.

The Times' editors recognized that missile defense was an area where the paper could provide unique news coverage based on exclusive source information. They gave me broad support to pursue this story. Because of the policy differences between the military and the political appointees, it became a great story for us. This is a good example of how you find good stories to report, whether breaking news or enterprisereporting.

In the end the dispute subsided—not ended—when the George W. Bush administration came into office. One of the first acts of the new administration was to jettison the 1972 ABM Treaty and begin developing not just short-range missile defenses, but long-range defenses against strategic missiles. Today, the United States is no long vulnerable to a limited long-range missile attack or an accidental launch. It has ground-based interceptors that can shoot them down. I feel satisfied that through my reporting on this area I made a significant contribution to America's national security.

Was I used by officials who wanted to win the policy debate? Yes. This is a fact of life in Washington. Reporters are used in numerous ways by power brokers and others. How does a reporter handle this? First, always keep in mind that you need to present both sides of the story. On controversial stories, oftentimes you will end up with lots of information on one side of an issue and paucity of facts on the other. You have to balance the reporting by presenting the other side, even if officials from the other side don't want to provide you with their side. This can be done be reporting what the other side believes and has stated in public, such as in congressional testimony or in speeches by officials, or by writings and other published materials outlining the issue.

7. TECHNICAL ASPECTS OF
WRITING A STORY

The final step in the reporting process is putting together a news story, having it edited and then published. Once you get your facts together and are confident you have confirmed the information through multiple sources, you are ready to put the story together. This can be a fast-paced process for a daily newspaper reporter and requires care. You must constantly balance two aspects: Content, or what you are saying, and basic English sentence, grammar and paragraph construction. A general rule for news reporting is to write one fact per paragraph, which can often result in one sentence paragraphs.

News stories begin with the lede sentence or sentences. Writing the lede is a critically important element of the story. The lede sets the tone for the rest of the story and will determine whether your story is read or ignored. If you lede is vague, chances are that no one will read the rest of it. If it is hard to understand, you lose readers. In the extreme, some editors tell reporters to write as if you are writing for 12-year-olds. The point is to make your lede and writing as clear and concise as possible.

Before writing the lede, think about what the headline would be for the story when it is published. This helps to capture the essence of your story in five to 10 words. The first step in lede writing is taking all the facts and information you have and figuring out what is the most important single piece of information you want to convey to readers. To do this, you need to know your subject.

One reporter once compared the process of writing a news story to filling up a bathtub with information. You load up the tub with facts and data and sort through it for the most important parts. When you're finished writing the story, you let the water out and begin filling up the tub for your next story.

Know your subject; this is far easier today, with the Internet and high-tech search engines, than when I first began reporting in the 1980s. Internet searches can be a relatively easy way to find out what has been reported before and what hasn't. Google it. If you see that your subject or lede has been done before, find a new angle or an angle that advances the story beyond what has been reported already. If your story has been reported by an obscure trade publication, again, look for new angles.

I have found Twitter to be an excellent vehicle for training on how to write ledes. Follow the top news organizations and you will see that Twitter's 140 characters, for news reporting, often are a combination of a headline and a shortened lede. Figuring out how to describe your story for Twitter is a good way to help focus your attention for writing the lede of the story.

Look for a compelling lead and write clearly and concisely. Tell the reader up front what you are going to tell them in the rest of the story. It may sound easy, but it is not. Always try to write clear leads. Follow the basic rules of writing: use active verbs over passive; favor the use simple instead of complex; make shorter sentences rather than longer ones. Read the classic 1918 writing handbook *The Elements of Style*, by William Strunk, Jr. and E.B. White. This is an essential guide to clear writing.

While writing your story, ask yourself questions: Is what I am saying clear? Can I make it clearer? Will the reader understand this? How can if alter the wording to make it better?

The news story begins with a lede and continues with more detail and less important parts further down. Use quotes. Quotes give life to a story, whether it is from a person commenting on the news in your story, or from a report with a particularly cogent or interesting statement. Sometimes I put a quote in the second paragraph after the lede. Quotes help the reader see that what you are reporting is from an original source and not the reporter. Avoid over-quoting. A quote should say something unique, rather than mundane. Often people's comments and report language are poorly written. So you as the reporter need to make what is said understandable by paraphrasing, and thus often correcting verbose or awkward English.

Again, write concisely. News organizations argue over readers' attentions spans. One school of thought says print media—to compete with the visual attractiveness of video—needs to produce very concise and short news stories. The second school says, the way to compete is to provide longer and more detailed accounts, the 'story-behind-the-story,' as a way to compete. The middle ground between these two news philosophies is probably the best approach.

How many words? Story lengths vary depending on the topic and the amount of information contained in the story. Long stories are usually investigative pieces that are chock full of details. It is up to editors to determine how much ink or electrons to devote to a particular story. For the Internet, 300 words is a good rule of thumb for a story. Now, try writing a 300-word story and you will see how difficult it can be to write concisely. It requires constant judgment about what is important and what is less important and can be left out. Most reporters want to tell everybody every little detail; experienced reporters, however, know that writing too long results in losing readers. If you do write long, try to break up the reporting into sections using subheads.

Feature writing requires reporters' more creative juices and usually an investment of more thought and care. Generally, features use an anecdote in the lede or the first few paragraphs as a device to attract the reader into the subject of your news story. Column writing is similar.

News reporting must remain free of opinions. Opinion articles are properly segregated, labeled and reported on the op-ed pages. Try to prevent "opinionizing" your story. For example, the use of the word "only" in news reporting can in some circumstances be viewed as a reporter infusing his or her opinion about someone or something. When writing, ask yourself, does my reporting sound neutral and unbiased?

My experience is that the key to good reporting is to tell the news story by letting the facts speak for themselves.

Comment by officials, experts and others related to your story is a good way to give life to your news stories. When reporting on complex defense or national security subjects, I often ask experts to give me a "what-it-all-means" quote. Remember that in reporting you are seeking to answer the basic who, what, when, where, why and how questions. Experts and people you quote often help reporters better explain the why of a subject.

Also, since your reporting likely will be around for a long time, make sure to address the "when" aspect of a story. Put in the day or date that something happened. News organizations in the past used the terms yesterday, today and tomorrow in time references but more and more dates are being substituted because of 24/7 publishing on Internet. Because of the Internet, many news organizations are shunning use of terms such as today, yesterday, this week, next month. Instead they date reporting with a specific date reference. For example, "The [specific event or element] took place Oct. 14 at the Baltimore Convention Center." The "where" question, like when often gets left out because reporters frequently are focused on answering the other questions.

Always remember to check the accuracy of details, like the spelling of people's names, and the spelling of specific places.

Style is set by each news organization, but one of the most widely used news styles is that of the Associated Press. Get a copy of the Associated Press stylebook and study it. A news organization's stylebook will include grammar, punctuation and spelling standards—like whether Moammar Gadhafi's name was spelled that way or Qaddafi, or many of the various ways that Arabic names are transliterated to English.

A SECRET TO SUCCESS

Finally, I want to leave with you a secret to success.

In my career I have found that one key to being a successful news reporter was that I have tried to help others. This is more than mutual back scratching. Whenever possible, I tried to assist people or organizations, sometimes with an expectation of a future benefit, and sometimes only with the hope that something good would come of it. This principle works amazingly well. Obviously, you should avoid being overly used. But don't worry too much about that. Reporters are frequently used by news sources. Always remember to keep your work and reporting within the confines of a professional "news perspective" and this principle will never produce any compromises.

My point to this secret of success is that you should never forget that doing good things for others is a practice that more often than not will return to you in a positive way in the future.

CONCLUSION

The news business is often a very unruly and competitive business. But for reporters in the United States, there is the tremendous advantage that American society is the most open and free society in the world.

Remember that the free press is a precious commodity and something that must be protected. Be aggressive but be responsible.

Approach your job as a news reporter as if you are someone engaged in the important profession of bringing news and information to people. Consider the news media as a public trust with the mission of ferreting out illicit activity. Be fair and always consider the potential impact of your reporting on people, good or bad.

In the end, use common sense and a sense of decency and propriety in your reporting. If you do, you will have a rewarding career.

APPENDIX:
WASHINGTON BY AGENCIES

Here are brief assessments of each of the main federal agencies in Washington and their relations with the press:

WHITE HOUSE
NATIONAL SECURITY COUNCIL

The White House is the pinnacle of the power structure in Washington and the target of major news coverage. White House correspondents regard themselves as in an elite class of reporters. They rarely break stories that are not fed to them by officials. The White House public affairs operation is usually the most politically charged of all the agency press operations. The National Security Council operates a parallel press office that is generally responsive to reporter inquiries. Email contact is possible directly with White House officials.

CONGRESS

The Congress operates press galleries for both the House and Senate that credential Capitol Hill reporters. Each member of Congress has a designated press secretary who is responsible for dealing with the press. Generally, members of

Congress are hungry for press coverage and thus press-friendly. Congressional staff on committee and member staff can be good sources.

DEPARTMENT OF DEFENSE ANDMILITARY SERVICES

The Pentagon is the largest federal agency in the Executive Branch and operates overlapping public affairs bureaucracies. The people in the Office of the Secretary of Defense (OSD) press operations are by and large unhelpful to reporters. In my over 25 years of dealing with this office I found them perhaps the most difficult to deal and the least helpful. The Joint Staff also has a press operation that is under the chairman of the Joint Chiefs of Staff. Each military service and several defense agencies also have their own press operations. Also, as the military is divided up into commands (Central Command, Pacific Command, etc.), each command has its own public affairs operations. This proliferation of press offices is structured so that each office can give reporters the run-around by telling them to call other offices to get the information, if the bureaucrat feels so inclined. A general rule is that the further away from Washington a public affairs office is, the more helpful it is. Email for OSD is [first-name].[lastname]@osd.mil.

The structure of the public affairs bureaucracy makes it essential for reporters to develop sources outside the official system.

DEPARTMENT OF STATE

The State Department is one of the more press friendly agencies. State Department press officers in my experience generally appear to help reporters obtain information and interviews, often arranging background interviews, albeit

slowly. The central press office is augmented by many direc-
torate-level press officers within the various State Department offices. State Department officials, posted in Washington and at U.S. embassies and consulates around the world
can be contacted directly using the email formula:

[lastname][firstnameinitial][middleinitial]@state.gov.

DIRECTOR OF NATIONAL INTELLIGENCE
CENTRAL INTELLIGENCE AGENCY
NATIONAL SECURITY AGENCY

The DNI was created to be an intelligence czar but in
recent years it has become almost a figurehead agency. The
DNI public affairs operation is generally unhelpful to reporters seeking news information. CIA has a very good press operation that is responsive to reporters' requests. As with most
agencies, when sensitive information is involved in an inquiry
they tend to decline to comment, usually with the indirect
formula of "I don't have anything for you on that." The National Security Agency, the largest U.S. spy agency, is perhaps
the least helpful public affairs operation. NSA is known for its
spying on reporters through a number of classified programs.
While technically illegal, no one has tried to hold the agency
accountable for its monitoring of U.S. reporters.

DEPARTMENT OF JUSTICE
FEDERAL BUREAU OF INVESTIGATION
DEPARTMENT OF HOMELAND SECURITY

The Justice Department public affairs office is usually
one that is politically-charged through the appointment of
political appointees who for the most part see themselves as
working for the attorney general and not the entire department. Justice officials will talk to reporters on background on

a limited basis, usually in connection with legal cases. The closer to the end of a case, the more accessible and open these officials become.

The FBI press office has a reputation for being unhelpful to reporters. Their officials tend to be spies seeking to learn what reporters are working on, rather than honest brokers who provide information to the press. Justice agencies like the Drug Enforcement Administration are better than main Justice and the FBI in terms of dealing with the press.

The Department of Homeland Security, a relatively new agency, also operates a large public affairs operation that again is usually politicized at the senior levels to focus on spinning and political damage control, rather than working to help reporters obtain information for stories.

DEPARTMENT OF ENERGY

This department during the 1990s was a major news generator, mainly as the result of nuclear spying cases. Energy public affairs officials can be classified as generally helpful to reporters, in answering queries and arranging interviews. DOE officials have helped in the past with provide exclusive material in advance of a major event, such as efforts to secure nuclear materials in unstable regions of the world.

SUPREME COURT
FEDERAL COURTS

The Supreme Court is one of the more difficult beats in Washington as most of its activities are carried out behind closed doors, until cases are argued before the court. Each of the Justices conducts their affairs very privately, rarely giving public speeches or giving interviews. The caution is based on concerns that justices will discuss matters that could eventually come before the court and thus they avoid contact, especially with reporters. I once met Justice Anton Scalia at a book-signing event and had a brief conversation with him. Supreme Court public affairs work with reporters on various court cases.

Federal Courts are open to reporters who cover trials and proceedings. Pacer, the official federal court document service, is an important tool for reporters who need to obtain court documents without having to go to each individual court.

LOBBYISTS AND INTEREST GROUPS

In Washington, it seems there is a lobbying and interest group for nearly everything, from wireless telephone service providers to candy makers. Lobbyists mainly target Congress and tend to shun the press, unless the press is used by lobbyists to advance their interest or the legislation they are working to pass. Interest groups are less formal lobbyists. They seek to promote certain particular interests, whether it is support for Israel (America Israel Public Affairs Committee) or conservative causes (American Conservative Union), or industries (American Gas Association). These groups can be valuable sources for reporters.